A small tortoiseshell feeding.

Pupa

Adult

Small tortoiseshell

The larvae eat stinging nettles in large groups which are easy to spot, and spin silk webs. Common in gardens.

3

Feeding on thistle.

Eggs

Larva

Pupa

Large white

The larvae are seen in large numbers in gardens eating cabbages. It is also called the cabbage white.

Eggs

Larva

A larva eating alder buckthorn.

Adult hatching

Pupa

Brimstone

Mostly seen flying along hedgerows or woodland edges. Brimstones hibernate, and can live for up to a year.

Egg

Larva

Pupa

Common blue with wings closed.

Male

Female

Common blue

The larvae feed on clovers and vetches which grow in downs and meadows. This is where the blue is often seen.

6

Egg

Larva

The female lays her eggs on grass.

Adult male

Pupa

Female

Meadow brown

The larvae live in long grass in winter, and the pupae hatch in June and August. The adult lives for only a month.

Egg

Larva

The red admiral loves
the juice of rotten fruit.

Adult
hatching

Pupa

Red admiral

A butterfly which
visits gardens from
May to October
The larvae live on
the leaves of the
stinging nettle.

Eating aphids on a rose bud.

aphid

Eggs

Larva

Adult

Pupa

Ladybird

Ladybirds can be found wherever aphids might be. They help the gardener by killing these pests.

Eggs

Egg hatching

Young bugs

Flying adult

Eating oak leaves.

Hawthorn shield bug

This colourful bug eats mainly oak leaves, hawthorn leaves and hawthorn berries, and is never found far from its food.

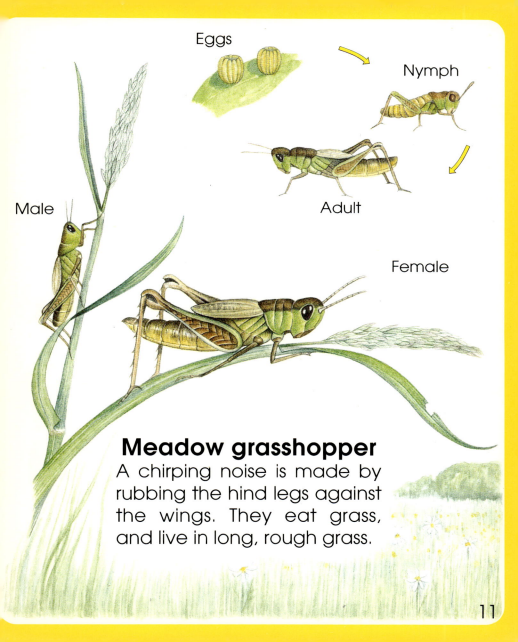

Eggs

Nymph

Adult

Male

Female

Meadow grasshopper

A chirping noise is made by rubbing the hind legs against the wings. They eat grass, and live in long, rough grass.

11

A bee collecting pollen from a foxglove.

A queen bee in her underground nest. She lays her eggs in wax cells.

Bumble bee

Bumble bee nests number about 150 bees. The workers collect pollen and nectar to feed to larvae in the nest.

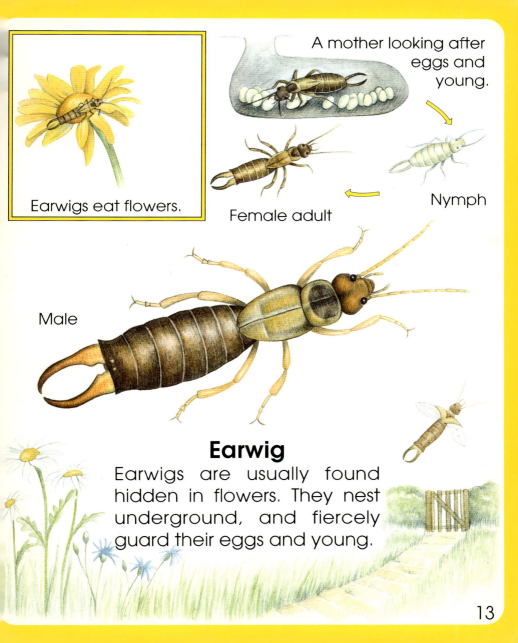

A mother looking after eggs and young.

Earwigs eat flowers.

Female adult

Nymph

Male

Earwig

Earwigs are usually found hidden in flowers. They nest underground, and fiercely guard their eggs and young.

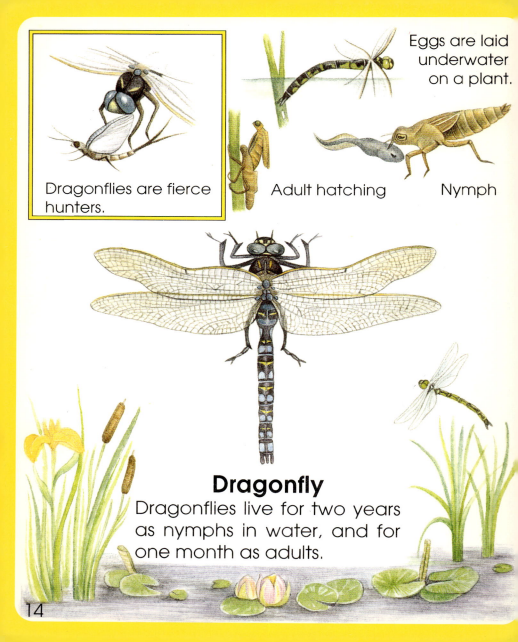

Dragonflies are fierce hunters.

Adult hatching

Nymph

Eggs are laid underwater on a plant.

Dragonfly

Dragonflies live for two years as nymphs in water, and for one month as adults.

Eggs

Larva

Pupa

Adult

The larvae eat many garden weeds.

Garden tiger moth

Although these moths only fly at night, their hairy larvae are often found in gardens in May and June.

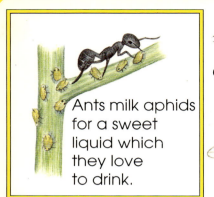

Ants milk aphids for a sweet liquid which they love to drink.

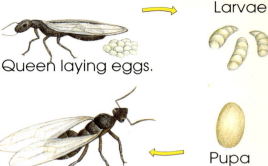

Queen laying eggs.

Larvae

Pupa

Adult queen

Worker ant

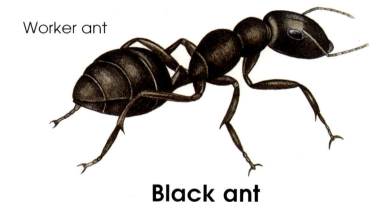

Black ant

Ant nests are common in gardens. There is a queen, and thousands of workers to look after her young.

Wasps love to eat jam ...

JAM

...and sweet, ripe fruit.

A wasps' nest in a loft.

Wasp

The queen wasp lays eggs in the nest. Other wasps look after her young and bring them insects to eat.

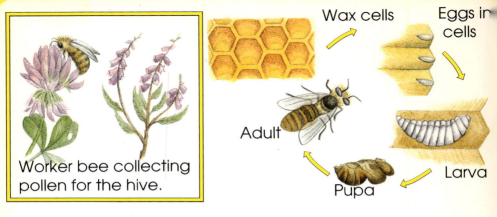

Wax cells

Eggs in cells

Adult

Pupa

Larva

Worker bee collecting pollen for the hive.

Honey bee

Worker bees collect pollen and nectar from flowers. This is made into honey in the hive where the queen lives.

18